Cavatinas for long nights

To Our Lady of the Aliases

Cavatinas
for long nights

Jim Christy

Ekstasis  Editions

National Library of Canada Cataloguing in Publication Data

Christy, Jim
  Cavatinas for long nights

  ISBN 1-896860-94-X

  I. Title.
  PS8555.H74C38 2001   C811'.54   C2001-911243-2
  PR9199.3.C4983C38 2001

© Jim Christy, 2001.
Cover Design: Miles Lowry
Author Photo: James Eke

Published in 2001 by:
Ekstasis Editions Canada Ltd.   Ekstasis Editions
Box 8474, Main Postal Outlet   Box 571
Victoria, B.C. V8W 3S1   Banff, Alberta ToL oC

Cavatinas for long nights has been published with the assistance of a grant from the
Canada Council and the Cultural Services Branch of British Columbia.

CONTENTS

I

Escondido Night

ESCONDIDO NIGHT

The moon is the shape
of this hidden cove
Fishing boats are constellations
We floated through a heaven
that glittered phosphorescent
like plankton in tinfoil
And paused between a pair:
Aurorita and Viridiana, to thrash
about like comets just
let out of school.
And continued on a light year
later   Moondust in my mouth
And all over your body

THE NEWS

The world arrives in a bundle
at First and Oaxaca, every afternoon
For a mere 6 pesos you get great
people and obscure dramas, earth-
shattering deals, heroics from
the playing field and a Question
of the Day. Augusto
Pinochet, and Gore and Bush. The
Palestinian leader and the Virgin
of Guadelupe. It's snowing in Toronto
and Calvin and Hobbes slide downhill
faster than Russians in Chechnya.

Benjamin Herera, aged 9, shot
Ciltali Sandoval, 7, who died
of a bullet in the neck an hour later
at a Red Cross hospital
in Hixltahuaca, Jalisco

Meanwhile at the Louvre
They're studying the science
of Ancient Make-up, An
Aussie Designer Rides Curves
and More Deals Could Be Sparked

The more and most beautiful models
We have for you. 5539-3949
Yummy Scandinavians. No mothers
of dead little girls. Or shrapnelled
Russian boys crying Mama Mama. Listen Leo
Be open-minded without being naive

Time-Warner has just merged with EMI
and a man walks by with his burro,
on this Puerto Escondido afternoon
in the good old-fashioned modern world.

JAGUAR WALKS

On the steps of Temple
Three, tourists arranged
In profile, stiff
As noble executioners
Each couple to a niche
Like a new-found glyph
Come to life

And at the far
Edge of it all sits
The bebidas man
With brown ancient eyes
And a tub full of Pepsis

The others are mouthing
Platitudes, snapping
Pictures, waxing spiritual
As in surrounding Ceiba trees
Toucans talk back

Holy Indigenes!
Holy Maya! Howler
Monkies mock Lonely
Planet chant—Holy
Holy are the People
None of whom ever
Made it up here
To this Esplanade of the Elite
Unless to serve as sacrifice

Over there the ballcourt where
High clan all-star teams
Played life or death games
With captives who were
Never informed of the rules

No dibble-stick maize farmers
In those tombs
Only numbers-mad murderers, priests
With penises perforated
By stingray spines, a status
Obsessed inbred oligarchy
Who squared the circle
Parcelled the heavens, and
From eunuchs received
Hallucinogenic enemas before
Lopping the heads off first-
Born virgins and getting down
To some good old Late-
High Classic Period
Necrophilia

They devised
The infallible Long Count
But not a way
To beat it

When the Park closes
Tourists rush for collectivos
To make the last plane for
Antigua. And
The bebidas man
Eternal indigene, heir
Of Temple slave labour
Shoulders his tub of Pepsis
And trudges off
As night rushes in to play
The jungle's music. And again
That jaguar walks

LIMELIGHT

He came round the promontory
baggy-suited from another era
duck-walking, churning sand in
vagabondo shoes while Mexican
vultures reeled so slowly
you thought they'd fall out
of a celluloid sky. Little Carlos
smiled at mudpie making muchachos,
tipped his topper, batted sad eyes
at pretty mothers and lost his topper
to a pregnant perro while deep
in an hidalgo bow.

Carlito fell ass over tea kettle
giving the Chihuahua chase
and got trapped in the middle
of a soccer game. Doing whirligig
whirls, kung fu kicks and pinball
pirouettes, he made accidental goals
with his hatless head. Exhausted,
Carlito flopped on a beach-lounger only
to be runoff by a hotel attendant
who was a ringer for old nemesis Mahatma
Kane Jeeves with bandileros and fake
moustachioes.

Fell in love with the blind girl
who sells platanos. Went
to Sierra Madres
in search of gold to pay
for an operation. Wound up
having to eat his huaraches. Was
a roller skating waiter in a Campeche
cantina. Raised chickens in Chichen Itza
Portrayed St. Nicholas
at Christmas on the Istmus
of Tehuentepec. Revived his old

music hall routines on Veracruz
vaudeville stages where no one laughed
Was kayoed by the champion mauler of Michoacan.
When Carlito came-to the wealthiest man in town
gave him money and a ride in his roadster
and had him arrested the next morning
when he'd sobered up

Little Carlos broke rocks on a Chiapan chaingang
but escaped through serpiente swamps. Assuming
the alias of Senor Verdad, Carlito murdered
a score of wealthy widows for their money,
And paid for the platano girl's operation.

You were there when they removed the bandages
and she got her first look, found
him no Antonio Banderas zorro hero
but just that bum in vagabondo shoes
And you saw his immortal look
recognizing her own. And Little Carlos
turned away. In his eyes the city lights
of Acapulco after a rain

She fell for the cellphone guy
who sold Ixtapa timeshares
and with a tip of the brim of a new
sombrero Carlito went his way,
baggy-suited, duck-walking
up the beach
at the crepuscular hour
into a setting sun, and back
to another era
that black and white one
where he belongs

VISIONS OF SUGAR PLUMS

Feliz Navidad
Best of the season
The gringoes have imported
their holiday. It's Xmas
in Mexico, Guatemala,
Maybe Nicaragua too
There's Santa Claus, a friend
of Jesus, I suppose, with
big belly, rosy cheeks
and Coca Cola by the fire-
place, stockings hung there
with care. Reindeer, they call
them, on the roof. But
I am of the colonias, just
a barefoot barrio boy. I shine
shoes but own nary a one. We do
our cooking on the floor
No fireplace. No
stockings to hang anyway
because we, all eleven of us,
are so poor. I want,
I want to go down to Acapulco
Maybe be a waiter, maybe dive
off La Quebrada cliffs. Haunt
the golden sands, meet
gringas who'll give me money. Later,
A gangster's life for me
I'll get rich and fat
like old St. Nick, buy presents,
wear shoes, drink coca cola,
fill stockings hung
by a fire

FLORES HOTEL ROOM AND LATER

What if one night in Guatemala
or anywhere, it turned out
to be true. Had to be because
all of a sudden there He is
in a Flores hotel room
You picture Him having walked
through the mercado smelling sewage
in ditches like everone else
Seeing the albino butcher, the woman crawling
like a scorpion, the guy with pants down
around his knees asleep on his stomach
in corn cobs and dog shit.
Watching everything
but saying nothing
because that's His game.
And you don't even notice Him unless
He wants you to. He would have
come over the Causeway
spooking caiman in the muddy evening shallows
Up sky blue tile steps. The blind
man on his penitent's chair
in front of the door to Number One, knew
who was pausing on the landing,
and mouthed His name. The dog in 106
barked which it hadn't done
in nine years, and the damn thing
wouldn't shut up. By the time
the bitch's mistress got over the shock,
she opened the door to a hallway empty
like scary movies. No footfalls
There wouldn't be though He walked.
And walked past the room where the woman lay,
door open, in a slip with lips
like she'd been eating pomegranates,
on a sheet the colour of faded tamarindo
He looked into the room
and into her heart and she came

for the last time and the first time
and when she was done felt pure, knew
no one would ever believe her but how
could she ever make anything like
that kind of money again.

So, yes, finally He's in your room
Just there is all. Down here
bus drivers invoke his name
before letting out the clutch
like disciples
on the outskirts of Emmaus

They call him El Senor,
and it is Him, no question, over
by your doorway. Inside
your Flores hotel room
and He's checking you out
You know who it is
Later somewhere else you'll hear
the questions, like: Was he wearing
sandals? A robe or what?
Was he white? They'll laugh,
people up there but not down here
these will cross themselves
kiss their hands and your hands
All you knew was Presence,
form indefinable, eyes and power,
and something filled the room
beyond all science knowing

Eleven days later in a fishing
village up the coast, the dog,
back and legs raw red, slimy
sores, putrescent shanks
poised shuddering at the curb
and of all the people chose
to look across the street at me
That same look, eyes

and power, presence, cool
beyond cool. And toppled over
to die in the gutter.

ILONIA IN ANTIQUA

Send your servant
At sweet siesta time,
To slip your note
Under my door. She
Needn't wait
For an answer. Sure,
I will be there. And,
Yes, we will make
Love most certainly. Call
Me your tresoro and I will
Call you mine.
But don't change your mind.
Don't go shopping, or get
Your hair done. Stay
Right there in your room
On your bed in naughty
Spanish lace. Make
Your ablutions,
Improper preparations,
Get ready, in other words,
To come not one
But two, three, six
Eight times, I can hardly
Wait. Send that note
If your husband
Won't be home
At sweet siesta time.

II

The Jazz Age

The Jazz Age

It's the Glen Island Casino
Just off the Shore Road not far
From the pretty little town
Of New Rochelle where the swing king
Is noodling his licorice stick.

I'm not dressed right, I tore my ducks,
Ripped my blazer up in Dedham,
The night Sacco and Vanzetti died.
But the wind from the Sound
Is ruffling your hair and your eyes
Are dancing in the June moon
Light.

         You're beautiful
As always
And I'm bugged as always
Because I can't explain what it is
About Benny, Les and Paul
And all those flaming young Gatsbys
Foxtrotting across a summer lawn
And because I can't, on the other
Hand, explain what it is
About Blue Devils and Basie.
I want to show you Pendergast's
Town where big bands are blowing
The blues right now, and Harry Truman's
A little judge in the backroom
Of the Spotlite nibbling
A pig's foot and a hooker's ear.
But you won't listen, and you
Won't go and it degenerates to squabbling
At three a.m. on the Old Shore Road
And ends only when

You thumb down the second trombone
With a boater and a flask
In a flivver and raccoon coat
And I turn west, travellin
Travellin all alone

THE STILL OF THE NIGHT

From a staircase atop a subway stop
somewhere doo wop is singing softly,
ropes and pulleys are squeaking as,
heavy and velvet, the rat-meal curtain
draws back   revealing rapscallion
players on an asphalt dumbshow
avenue of a stage, rowhouses either side,
like redbrick tombstones

See three urchinly little larrikins
tossing pieces of curbside toward the back
of a grown up man who dared come here
from some other neighborhood. Affronted
by such a display of audacity, the ir-
repressible tykes feel it incumbent upon
themselves   to take it out on his hide
And would kick his corpse all the way north
to South Street, if they had a mind
to be nasty and the night was not still young
and a better life   waiting underground

The mameluke lost his fedora in the gutter
at the front of the house of the push-
cart man. The gambler from 827'll
find an overcoat with a Lit Brothers label
on his stoop when from a 3am taxi he alights

Does the staggering interloper have a wife
somewhere, some saucy frail who's
missing him maybe? this man
in a blue serge suit.

      Will he be a goner or
      Make it to the corner?

We let him live, I think
See, we only knew our lines
and not the gist of the thing

Keys and cufflinks, tatters
of fabric and drops of blood,
slivers of skin and hanks of hair
are scattered like glass at a car
crash, up and down our sorry-ass set

Now the rat-meal curtain's closing
and we reach up to pull
the manhole covers to.
Some guys harmonize *In the Still
of the Night,* and we slip back
to a better life, waiting
underground

NINETY DAYS

Heard a faint siren as
At midnight in the middle
Northern latitudes I lay me
Down in the long grass meadow
Shadowy forms of ranchhouse
Suburbia way over there. A piece
Of long grass meadow `tween
My teeth. Hands—fingers
Under head entwined—my pillow.

Stared at Constellations—the siren's
Arc like a comet coming my way
But evil deeds and perpetrators seeming
Unreal somehow from here

I dozed and dreamed me Hercules
In love, breathing the hair
Of Berenice, and Dixie Louise
Snuggling up to me
While lyres played under
The Avalokitesvara diamond
Skies of heaven's Bedouin camp

SUDDENLY
Lights brighter than Betelguese
Blinding my eyes
And big cops to kick
And Orion-club me,
Throw my idling ass
In the Draco-net squad car.
Downtown they made like Castor
And Pollux, you know,
The bad-cop worse-cop routine.
Boxed my ears and finally
Booked me ninety days
For being
                    starry-eyed

A NIGHT IN THE TOMBS, 1968

It wasn't the transvestite
six-foot five, black and bent
on fellatio, nor the other
Brothers: the armed robber
and a guy who'd just killed his wife,
that I minded. No, it was
the white guy, small,
skinny with greasy hair. He
might have been preaching Love
in Tompkins Square, save for eyes
like grey glass in dishwater frozen.

"Listen, I'm in the head," he says
"Chinese restaurant down on Canal
Street? Finish pissing and the nigger
comes in, gives me a shoulder.
Signifying, you know. Goes over
to the urinal, says, 'Sheeit!'
and turns on me, his ugly dick out
'Pick your butt out the urinal,
so's I can piss, honkey.' I start
to leave. 'Hear me, muhfuck?' I say,
'No way'and reach the door. He
comes after me, his
dick flapping."

Our cellmates regarded him with serious
concentration, except for the guy
who'd killed his wife. He
was sobbing.

"And he grabs me by the neck,
forces me to the pisser, pushes
my head down. What I do is I
get the knife from my boot,
reach around and stick it
in his side. The nigger,

he jumps back and I shove
the blade between his shirt buttons,
all the way in. You should have
seen the look on his face. Then I
cut off his dick,
I did."

Two guys in uniform came for me
and another pair in suits
worked me over
in the elevator on
the way up to the courtroom.
And while justice
was being meted out to me.
I thought of him down there
getting his.

To John Still In The Joint

Yo, bro.
Was this little bird
whispered in my ear, just
the other day Said you did
jack jump up
before the parole board
once again and once again
the good citizens stuffed you
back in the box which means I think
there's still another deuce to do
on account of your attempt to make
it over the wall. Did you really
think they'd mistake
your laundry for your sorry
ass sleeping self
under the threadbare blanket?
Tough luck, dude.

Now we're all wise to another kind of bird
One that whispers in the wrong ear
sings a twisted song's what I'm
saying, hoping to feather his own nest.
But that ain't you, Homes, as everybody
knows. So I raise my glass. You're
a real Johnson, John. But
better you than me.

Oh, as for the bikini babes
on the beach on the front
of the card? There're here
right now and we're all under
the third palapa from the left
and my girl is just setting down
the Carlo Suarez, the lime and salt
Sorry, to rub it in, bro.
So what am I doing here? They
let me out the day before Ty Conn

got his. Yeah, it was a year
early but that's, shall we say,
another story. Anyway, just like
the pirate captain done, this
kid went right to the 'X' and now
I'm south of the border living large
Just proves that crime does pay
for some of us.

And my new squeeze? The one that just
brought me the tequilla? I know you
won't mind me saying it's a certain
someone who's been your
old lady too and turns out
wasn't such a changed chick
afterall. Same old Mary. She never
married the scripture study fellow.
Didn't get Jesse back from MHR
But Mary Mainline doesn't dine
at the dumpster any more, wear
kneepads neither not since
she's got an old man knows
how to take care of her, introduce
her to silk and Prime Ministers. Which
don't change the fact that
if I said trick the bitch would
turn it.

Well that's all for now, dude.
The coconut oil keeps running
into my eyes. It's only time,
John. Do those days
one by one. Adios, sucker.
Signed,
A Rat
in Margaritaville.

FAST COMPANY

Hanging out with Joe Albany
on a Tickletoe October afternoon,
tripping through trash-tossed lots
between Tenth Avenue tenements.
John D. Robinson joins in
doing majorette tricks
with drumsticks

We're in an apartment somewhere
Joe at the piano, John on traps,
Hudson River out the window.
Guys from Woody Shaw's band fall by.
One with an alto, another bass guitar
And suddenly it's Autumn
in New York

Next day Joe recalls Bird
and Camarillo, Pres,
Warne Marsh. And legendary now
livingroom recordings.
Shows photos, one in Toronto
on the grass of a park,
late-Twenties with his uncle
a chef at the King Edward

That night, on 116th Street,
the West End Bar, and a quartet.
Laura, Sweet Lorraine and Love for Sale
Howard McGhee, his trumpet muted
Surprised I know who he is, and
Sticks and Brownie, his brothers
Papa Joe Jones rests his old arm
on my shoulder, tells a story.
Me suprised to be there.
At last among immortals

IF YOU CAN'T SEE MY MIRRORS,
I CAN'T SEE YOU

Rolled through Rico, just over
the Alabama line. Crackers in August
with eyes like skinned knuckles
sitting and spitting, cottonmouths
have come out from under porches
to change places with coon-hunting dogs

The past is roaring down on me
like a White Freightliner straddling
the center line, avoiding every airbrake
check point, hauling more
than the legal limit of reminders

We passed this way once, headed
to Surrency, Social Circle
or Swainsboro. Picnic glades,
motor courts and even roadside weeds
have their sweaty secrets, way stops
all, on our private highway to Splitsville

Indeed, I was your swain and you made
even me blush, our social circle
shrank to you and me and ours, and a few
weeks' worth of motel clerks
and package store employees

I'm out in the countryside now, you're in
the sideview mirror and, of course, there's
the rearview which started it all, walking
across a party floor in Weehawken
in that jersey dress at least
a size too small

Here the earth is the colour
of all the cheap wine we drank. And
then there was the time…But, never mind,
I'd best step on the gas, accelerate
out of the kudzu tangle of the past
and into a not nearly so naughty now.

HIGH PLAINS DRIFTER

He leaned forward in the saddle
as if on the horns of a dilemma
An outlaw by experience
but to beauty inclined.
He'd been drifting the high plains
for as long as even
wizened mountain men remembered
leaving bits of legend, like spent
cartridges, in low-ceilinged
saloons from Mexicali
to Medicine Hat. And he always
went in wondering who at what
table or which one at the bar
would try and fill his hand
And one of them usually did
But never soon enough

And times in his bedroll,
the big chestnut in the mesquite
hobbled, fetlocks like she'd waded
through whitewash, he'd picture
how it was, the blunt
burnt powder smell. A table
turned over and some sharp's
aces and eights scattered over the floor
Those double doors still swinging
after they dragged the body out

Memories aplenty there were
in those silver-studded saddlebags
Schoolmarms, ranchers' daughters,
and a chorus line of dancehall girls
with holes in their dirty bloomers
who all needed a bath—they might
have filled a train of conestoga wagons

Then came the War, and he broke
out of Andersonville, travelling north
at night, making New York City, going
incognito and underground, emerging
to dine at Delmonico's the night
they brought news of Appomatox
And seen in the celebation
amid fireworks and confetti
in crinoline and ribbons
the girl in the hansom

Washington Square promenades
days and nights of strolling, cabs
and the opera, giving her jewelry
that wasn't stolen. Lily Langtry,
gas lamps and oriental carpets
Paintings of a rainy Paris, daguerrotypes
and steriopticons in the parlour. All
as if he'd never killed a Kiowa
or robbed the Wichita Stage

And yet he'd left her narrow house
and wide four-poster of perfumed sheets
Rode the train to St. Joe, crossed
the Big Muddy in his outfit
and loped into open country
But it wasn't til he gunned down
that scrofolous trail bum
in Abilene—who'd tried to steal
the ivory-handled buttonhook
she'd used to take off her
slender shoes—that he felt right again

A score more years of it
But what's a man like him to do?
Wyatt refereeing prize fights in Colima
Masterson back east working for
a paper. He'd turned down Hickock
at least a dozen times. And Buffalo
Bill'd never spoken to him
since that night on the Three Forks River
No, he'd just keep drifting, adding
chapters to the dime novel version
of himself. Laying waste more
mothers' sons. Until some night
just like this one while he drowsed
with saddlebags for a pillow under
a commanche moon and a buffalo
blanket of stars, he finally wasn't
quick enough when the end came at last
in the form of a half-breed he'd offended
in Denver and didn't even remember

Some drifter disguised as death
who'd lie about it
to Ned Buntline later

ARTHUR AND THE JAWS OF IGNOMINY

Hey, Rimbaud. I thought of you
today. Saw a ride like the one
you used to wheel. A '51
Mercury, two-door, black, dropped
with chopped top. I pulled over
for a closer look but, no, it
was a show car, and my old buddy'd
never own that kind
of short. Yours was pocked
and primered, rusting around
the rocker panels. I remember
you pulling up to the house
that last time, onto the lawn.
The Merc pinged and sighed.
The house was in Toronto but
in North Florida, too. The night
was full of crickets
and fireflies. We both wore
t-shirts. Marlyn's blouse
was open, lace bra underneath.
You saw me see you look. "What
ever was I thinking?" you thought
out loud. "You know, Verlaine
and all that." I replied
that you were just a kid.

We sat on the porch, ate mescaline
The tops of hydrangea bushes
were rolling purple hills, pink, maroon
and blue. You named them A and E,
and I and U. We watched the sky
turn colours too, the clouds question
and exclaim. Then Marlyn passed out
and we got in the Merc. The tattered
headliner tickled my ear as we tore
down the two-lane, radio turned up, us
denting the dashboard with early

Ellington. "It's like the music
they played behind early mouse
adventures," you said, and I pictured
cartoon cannibals hot-footing it
across savannahs of Africa with bones
in their noses, girls with bouncing
midriffs wrapped by feather tufts
like Queen Ann's lacey ruff. And
here comes, caught in the highbeams
on the highway before scurrying
into sun-scorched vision plains—
Jimmy Rushing with his spear
and strange designs on the wildebeeste
skin of his shield, like quarter note
clusters. He looks embarrassed, Mister
Five by Five, like a costume extra
who wandered off the set.

"Didn't see nothing like that, my part
of Africa," you said. We drove all night
Radio guys pitching five-piece living
room groupings. You recalled Charleville
bourgeois parlours. Sudanese clayhuts
Working the docks at Bremerhaven. We swapped
yarns, traded jackpots, hooked up with two
black girls not in the snows of Paris
but the Gator Club, Washington Street, Saint
Augustine. I saw you doodle on a napkin, asked
if you ever wrote anymore, even half a line
of a poem on the back of a ship's manifest.
You shook your head, said you'd had it
with that shit long ago. "I was snatched
from the jaws of ignominy   just in time."

We got jobs as snake handlers, swept
out a whore house in Perpignon. Did
a week in the cooler in Kelowna. Sold
Kalishnikovs to some Levantines
who turned around and shot each other.

It was the funniest thing.   But we
came a cropper in Marseille.
Had to lie doggo in a warehouse
on the docks. No, not at the Vieux Port
you used to know. These are way to hell
and gone. Doctors diagnosed
gangrene. Academy members wouldn't have
anything to do with you so it fell to me
to do the cutting. You never made a sound
as I hacked and chopped, just kept smoking.
Blood and puss spurting every which way. But
what's a friend to do, eh? I got
the jesus thing off and sewed
up the stump with the sharpened end
of a peavy.   After
laying up a few days, you got in the Merc
and started her up. "Life," you said
out the window.,"is the farce we all
have to perform."   And drove away.
back to whatever dream you came from.

And I sold the leg
to the University of Texas.

CONTINENTAL DIVIDE

Come over the Divide, first time
Stepping down from a semi in the October
Afternoon, hiking along a two-lane
Through a bowl of forest ringed round
By Rockies. A roadhouse
With a barbecue hut ahead
Child's crayon swirls of chimney smoke
Against a pale pure blue sky

Inside a young crewcut white man
In fat overalls, three rows of boilermaker
Fixins lined up along the mahogony
Shotglass of Old Overholt, a thimble
in lobster claws. A sleeve of beer
Follows. He leans back his melon head
voice deepens to a rumble

                                    They call it...

Someone "Oh, yeah"'s encouragement

                                    Stormy Monday
But Tuesday's...

Just ten or twelve in there, all know
The big boy is special, has this
Wondrous voice and wonder why
He must muscle that '47 flathead
Flatbed Dodge through the gears of day-to-day

                                    Thursdays
Also sad...

They stand him a beer and a shot
After every song, and the rows
Deepen with the blues, Talk About Me
Woke Up This Morning Tomorrow Night
He changes West Coast to Rocky Mountain

Lover then it's back to Stormy Monday on
A sunny Wednesday afternoon
At a roadhouse just outside Denver
In a bowl of woods ringed by Rockies,
Before the War was on everybody's lips
No suburbs there yet. No town or school
named for five clusters of daisies, no
Students wielding guns
Just those old-time blues

Tacos of Eternity

Lexington, June,
1966. In town too early
For hospital visiting, I
Walked across the campus
Jocks, three in a car by the old
gridiron, tumbled out with bristling
heads and beady-eyed anger
because, because I was some
hipster or homo or hobohemian
or from up north or just because.
And the police came, and
it was me they took away,
because of one or all the above.
The cell wasn't bad
with its barred view
of an asphalt lane and brownbrick
building, merging in memory
with a counterpart somewhere
I didn't ponder injustice but dreamed
of that woman back home, ten years
older, some Italian guy's blond
wife she wore silk
stockings held up by belt
and garters like many
still did those days.
and had thick hair below her waist
and didn't shave til mid thigh, the straps
like blacktop country roads
through dun prairies west of there.
"He'll kill us if he finds out," she'd say.

The next afternoon, I took a taxi
to the hospital where legends
used to go for the cure. There was
an experimental farm and a two-
Headed cow, and it made you
wonder what they tried

43

on the junkies. They brought
Charlie out in tennis shoes,
white t-shirt, khakis. "Oh, man,"
he groaned; for him, enthusiasm.
He had a chair, I had a chair,
and a large guard was right there.

CL talked about Alexander King
in the same wing in '49 or
Fifty, about Chet; playing
bass with Buddy Rich on Tacos,
Enchiladas and Beans
And when he said he'd
gotten caught just a month ago
with percodans in his pocket
and a mouth full of pills
in a drugstore that happened
to be closed at the time, I
leaned close, and Charlie,
nodding at the fat guard, said
"Oh, he's heard everything." There
On the linoleum floor,
in the sunlit dayroom
of Kentucky eternity

BLUESAVENUE

She slipped out of the Forlorn Arms
and fled across the town square
while I was making the liquor store
run, and I returned to a room
scented by Chanel and cigars—hers.
And the sheets looked like Death Valley

"She broke a heel, crossing the lobby," said
the bellhop, a nasty hophead dressed in black.
"The one-eyed tramp, the baby-talking
trollop, unmentionables sticking
out of her cheap valise for God
and all the world to see."
Yeah, and I bet He or She
or It didn't mind for a moment.

"There's only one place they run,
types like that," he added. "And only
a chump like you would follow."

It had been raining forty nights,
and I started my search from the back seat
of a Yellow Ark to Nowheresville
The Guatemalan cabby crossed himself,
as if knowing what awaited
when he pulled up
to Bluesavenue

I stuck a tentative kick out
and down and directly into
a neon chartreuse puddle. And
from an afterhours juke joint
I somehow knew I'd never find,
it being outside space, far beyond
Time, Chu Berry with his trumpet
tugged my benny, told me
I didn't have a ghost of a chance.

Dry ice spilled from manhole covers.
One-hit wonders slept in doorways, also-rans
in gutters, has-beens hunkered in the shadows.
Street signs warned: Go Back! and no matter
how much I bribed the parking metres they
never changed their tune:
Your time's up, man!

Still I staggered forth along
This boulevard of broken
you-know-whats, strictly
a one-way street, tracking,
inspite of myself, a gaudy dream
in gauzy bombazine

The tires of a cop car
cruising in the rain
made a sound like Marlene
Dietrich crossing her legs.
Hell, I'll tell anyone who'll listen
she was nothing compared to you—blue angel,
blonde venus, scarlet empress, ruler of my heart.

For a plugged nickel I'd reiterate your charms
to those old boys leaning
on the paper boxes waiting
to take the early edition back to little rooms.
But they only want to listen
to hissing radiators that remind them

of the shrewish dead wives they hated for decades.
Some guys'll get sentimental over anything

And on the dumbshow avenue floats roll by
with vignettes from our ill-starred affair,
a brief episode that like an ass I've been
drinking to the end of for donkey's years.
There's the one where I sprung you in Dubrovnik
after they pumped your stomach and doctors
in Croatian discussed your configuration.
I told you you should have worn clean underwear.
I told you you should have worn some underwear.

And now the bloody architecture's
taken on a horrible human physiognomy.
Between bricks, the mortar's weeping
And you're in every cornice of my eye
Woman, you've been
the devil's doorway. Every
knob and keyhole remind me
of what I want to do to you.
Maybe there's
something from you in those letter slots.
Rooftops invite me to leap.
The hookers all look like they should
be holding up gables, one in cheap
Russian shoes with red-painted,
gargoyle-pointed toenails promises
nasty doings in non-existent backseats
Hell, she can't even afford
the Ladas in her stockings.

Come back,
I'll do the cooking honey; I'll
be your man, scrub the floor
and score all the percodans you could
ever want. Where are you?
Ah, probably flat on your back somewhere
Maybe it's in an alley and you're tossing empty

bottles at the moon, trading fours with tom cats,
tripping a trash can hi-hat, reciting a litany
of your former husbands. Christ!
you'll be there all week.

But…
I've reached the end
of the Avenue and my tether
Nothing ahead except a deadend and
the abbatoir. There's
the street-sweeping guy
his broom like snare drum brushes
The milkman's in his wake, death
rattles in his bottles, and Pepper Adams
is doing Life's
a Son-of-Bitch. When they
bring out the baritone,
I know it's time to slink back home

And here now's the Forlorn Arms
and the town square looks alot
like me. Guess I'll knock
that pimp, that pirate, that preacher,
that pilot, that poet off his plinth
climb up there and call myself
Just Another   Victim
of the Blues

ALL THAT REMAINS OF CHICKIE NARDUCCI

There are no   Sufis in South
Philadelphia where even a protestant's
shit out of luck

Yeah, I know: You can't go you-know-where
again and a fellow shouldn't even try. Yet
there I was wheeling a rental
through that familiar foreign territory.

They don't get tourists
south of the liberty bell
So your identity better be
stamped on your face. Look
like you know it all and nobody'll
ever put one over on you.
If you're questioned, just claim you grew
up on Morris Street or Montrose
And you've got to move
on account of slant-eyes
have made it to Washington Avenue
and the spear-chuckers are creeping
closer and closer.

They left the tracks but took away
the trolley. All around are rowhouse
windows still empty as a loanshark's
eyes. And they haven't moved,
those kitchen-chair goombahs
on the streetcorners. They'll kiss
their crucifixes prior
to kicking your ass

I'm at Christian and Passyunk
where my favourite uncle, Uncle
Ange drew five in the chest
while pulling his last Blue Ribbon.
God, he made great sauce. And, see there?

49

Above the olive oil importer?
that's the flat where Mario
Lanza hid out, his mother
feeding him too many cannolis
before wise guys
pulled out his tubes.

Reese Street, Catherine and Ritner
Streets I didn't know were deforming me
All those bad B movies transpiring
on an asphalt screen in a red brick theatre
with the exits chained and locked.

All the ones gunned down
trying to get made and others
who lammed it to the other side
of the Delaware but found
nothing over there cause
you can take him or her
out of South Philadelphia
but you can never—ah,
the hell with it

I said my last arrivaderci
from a vinyl backbooth
getting the old mal occhio
from soldiers in a world grown
small ever since the Gentle Don—
they used to call him Lindbergh—
got a Snyder Avenue makeover
that never messed the naughahyde
but did inaugurate the blood bath
decade that followed. And even now
that may not be hot sausage I'm eating
at this table in Cous' but all
that remains of Chickie Narducci.

I could hardly keep from
crying in the cannelloni

I avoided the eyes
that followed me to the door
Gave my money to the lady
with the wig and the rhinestone glasses
—I think we used to do things in alleys
back when Dilworth was mayor
and Ike in the White House—
and hit the streets
where no stickball ragamuffins
were breaking windows

But the goombah homeguard were still
on crumbling corners with small-of-the-back
pieces, protecting the nothing-much that is left
from yellows and blacks and anglo saxons

So I buckled up my rental and headed west
Trying to stay true   in the tracks
of that long-gone trolley

How Deep Is The Ocean?

Hey, man. Dig
the old hipster
mumbling about the ocean to a vodka neat
He took to the sauce when he fell
off the Horse when he got too old
to score

Fall by there and stand him a double,
he's sure to pull your coat
about those long gone real
gone nights back before jazz
went to college and he still
had his chops

He shook more than just a couple
of jolts and was given
to falling out in the street.
The man owned every side
Lennie Tristano ever made
Knew Billie personally. Dizzy
too, and Mezz and Pres,
Bags and Bean, Slim and Slam
and Django and Jug. Not to mention
Thelonius Monk.

Man, you only think the cat's
at that table all alone. In his mind
he's deep in a sentimental journey
back on the Basie bus, jamming
cross all of Indiana

That old scene's all
he's got eyes for recalling
With trumpet summits and cutting sessions
like other men's beachheads
and bombing runs. Yeah, man;
he was one of the session soldiers

marching like wigged-out Souzas
in back of Bird, when Platoon Leader
Parker took that bridge; you know,
the one in Cherokee

Where'd they go, those languid
cocktail lounge ladies who blew
lazy smoke rings toward the bandstand
with messages like melodies in bop, implied?

Who was that vined down young hepcat
at the corner of Lex and a Hundred and Ten?
Could this sorry party in a mouldy pork pie
and threadbare box back benny
be he
Sitting alone
at a table
bad music on the box, over
where the stage used to be
mumbling to a vodka neat
about how deep,
how deep is the ocean? The one
that will swallow him,
and me, and you,
man?

WAY NORTH JAZZ

You can have your springtime in Vermont
Dawson City round about December's for me
Summertime, the playing's
too easy at Newport or Nice
And what could be more obvious
Than Autumn in New York

The miraculous buds of May—
August evenings on porch swings—
Kicking leaves in russet October—
All like smudged pages from a fake book
Of Dixieland standards pawed over
By a wedding reception quartet
Who all have day jobs down
At the mill

Give me some way north jazz
From a combo of glacial cool
Blowing choruses transparent
As blue ice, clean
As snow crust reflecting
A moon like frozen butter

The drummer's kit's of Caribou
Skin, his sticks Stalagtites.
The bass player's grown polar bear
Claws. Saliva on the tenorman's
Reed turned to ice at forty below
The trumpet's lips are stuck
To his mouthpiece so
They'll have to keep playing
And playing, their set extending
Until someday they'll be found
Suspended in mid-chorus
In a glacier, their notes, frozen
In time

III

Spadina Doughnuts

SPADINA DOUGHNUTS

Early first Canada Day in the new country
and already the joint's filled
with bleary-eyed early holiday
risers munching sinkers, night owls
in wrinkled fancy threads afraid
to go home, and a few off the stroll
barely advertising. The counter girl
looks like Charles Bronson, hands me
a cup and a menu that reads like
a brothel's bill of fare:
Cream Dream, Ravishing Sweets, Jelly
and Juicy   Every doughnut sounding like
something you'd take to a hot-sheet motel.

Over there an Afro-topped kid in felony shoes
whispers in the ear of a yellow-headed woman
who's lived fifty hard winters. She merely
blinks at his propositions, about as surprised
as a barn owl, smirks, probably thinking, "My
kid's older'n him but why'n hell not?"
In a corner by the out-of-order washrooms
three old fillies discuss the ponies and the
white-haired, white-bearded birth-marked man
at the next table. "Christ," one biddy mutters,
"he reminds me of a powdered doughnut oozing
raspberry filling."

Nearby, the world's oldest convicted thief,
Ace Miller's selling winter overcoats, "an
off-season special," he says. And the Gimp,
his protegeé a second-story man, who shattered
his pelvis in a third-story fall, clutching
a Toshiba all the way to the sidewalk.
"Yeah, man," he says, "but
I got a double sawbuck for the tube."

There're no patriot flag wavers in here only
lamsters, shamsters, disbarred shysters and one
homosexual private eye. All you have to do
is keep your forehead off the formica, like
Silent Sol at the corner of the counter dipping
a cruller in his cup continually
like an oil derrick in Alberta

The greasy door opens. I watch the cop come in
and Ace Miller sees Mimico. Off comes the cap
from woman's hair. Dark blue slacks render
the rear end androgynous. She looks around
with cop eyes but hers are for only doughnuts,
And leaves with a bag of assorted
as the joint sighs.

And soon the sun comes up over chimney pots
signalling a change of shift, so
the kid hits the bricks with the bottle-blond,
fillies leave with the Form and I slide out,
arm in arm with Mocha Sweetie, my very own
holiday treat with strawberry,
melt-in-your-mouth lips and cherry red heels.

A Lush In Garters

Through the drizzle of Saturday afternoon,
the airport bus shuttled me into a town
where at every intersection memories
lurked like muggers. I called
at the Pilot Tavern which wasn't
where it used to be but I had
turned a corner too. And so had she
by the look of her, the good looks
of her vanished, like all those
Presbyterians just a reminder now
at the bottom of a glass.

Jazz music was playing, some rag-tag
quintet, and she was nodding in time like
the last time and a thousand other times.
Her hair still luxurious though chestnut
no more, green eyes in nests of wrinkles
still insinuating. That young simper replaced
by a smirk of a certain age. And the first thing
she said was the same as the last thing
she'd said, "You going to buy me a drink?"

So I did what I'd done back then, and she
told the man to make it a double.
"Well what have you been up to?" I asked
"Oh," she replied, "I've been leading
a lush life in some big towns."
And she thrust forward breasts
that weren't quite where they used to be,
adding, "Me and the trombone player,
we called it quits."

"I thought you were with that piano guy?"
I said, and she said oh that was
ancient history. "I've gone through
an entire goddamned orchestra since then."
And she curled her lip and ordered another one.

"You look a lot older," she said
"I am," I replied.
"We had a good run. You and me."
"Yeah," I answered. "A good run."
She leaned back in the chair
and crossed her legs, nail polish
gloss on stocking runs. The legs,
I had to admit, were the last to go.

Meanwhile the band went on The Hunt,
alto squawking and tenor honking,
frantic like fighting cocks;
behind the drum kit was a spastic
whipping egg whites; the bass player
had Churchill cigars instead
of fingers; and that piano guy,
he was only pretending to be blind,
digging her stems in back
of George Shearing-shades

"We could play that tune again, you know,"
she said. "I've forgotten how it goes,"
was my reply. And she crossed them higher,
letting me see whatever I cared to see,
which was mainly that she   was
one of the last of a breed that
still wore garters. Her muttering,
"In case you need a reminder."

I turned my head and there was a fat guy
in a Clifford Brown t-shirt looking hard
at where I had only glanced.
She indicated we could
call a cab and grab a bottle
on the way back to her place
where she was certain she could
help me get back my once familar
embouchure. I said I had to go,
and she said, "Hey,

I'm not one to insist on condoms."
I got up, put money on the table. She looked
at it, asked, "You're not still
with that Puerto Rican cutie, for chrissakes?"
"She was Mexican," I said.
"Hell's the difference?"
When I told her so long, she said "Yeah,
vaya con fucking dios."—and began
culling the tip.

I looked back when I reached the door.
Clifford Brown was starting to make his move.
Nothing in this life like a lady in distress,
especially a lush in garters
with her skirt up to there.

PARADISE THREADS

He looks
like the monk who
makes the wine
With bald pate, haloed
head of dirty curls
The Saturday Star
a pillow on
his concrete cot
Burn victim ankles
swollen and shiny
Line of spittle on his lips
Fifty-something, some
old pensioner's Sonny Boy
Unseen by tanktop narcissists
sipping protein shakes
on the way to the Bull Dog Gym
He opens eyes the colour
of the dishwater sky
Opens too a mouth of stumps
but makes no funny,
says nothing pithy. Mumbles,
gurgles, passes out
again in the doorway
of a bankrupt Paradise

WITH MY EYES WIDE OPEN

Warm Ottawa October
By flagstone mosaic walk
Under the backyard maple
Twenty-nine years to
The day later, reading
Little dharma pops
Hearing basketball thumps
On leafy macadam
A voice perdurable against
Everybody's end

What became of Sue who loved
The moustached lady
In the Sparks Street store?
Where's the Greek who slept on couch
All of Autumn's afternoons
That nineteen sixty-eight?
And Margie's serious Zairean student, he
Now Fifty-some year old
Cabinet minister from Congo?

MacKelvie on Cooper Street,
The canal and Moody Lake,
Red Gatineau hills,
And the Government too
Still there.
I've returned, a visitor
Ignorant of the truth
That emptiness is all—or,
So it says—that
Matters. And verily Life
Is but a dream.

TORONTO TODAY

Ten floors above a march against
violence and cutbacks. Hotel
window wrapped in a sky the exact blue
of old Chinese roominghouses. Looking
down on tar-topped roofs, a plastic
orange tarp trapped between vent
and chimney, beach chairs on pallets,
potted forgotten annuals. There's
a man sweeping a concrete store
backyard. Thick wavy black hair, head
lifts, reveals gentle sportshirt belly

On the other side of the street
and a few buildings to the south
a woman's hitting at a rug
on a clothesline with a broom, hands
apart like a batter from the deadball
era. She stops. Do her shoulders heave?
I wave futilely as she tilts back
her head, catches city sun on Greek
or Portuguese face.

The man meanwhile also stops, lights
a smoke and leans on his broom. I imagine
him exhaling with a long sigh, thinking
of his brothers back in Thessalonia

Man and woman on opposite sides oblivious
to the chanting snake that has Saturday
off, and writhes between them on Yonge Street.
Stamp out this and sweep away that. The
snake hypnotized by unblinking eyes
of the Evening News

Now Playing

It's some kind of crazy
comedy, guaranteed to make you
laugh and cry. All about two
ill-starred and aging romantics. One
driving west while you
fly east. A devilish dj taunting
with Ben Webster soundtrack.
Now it's the Nearness of You,
as the 401 unreels a selection
of your greatest performances
from the last forty-eight hours

Those aren't grey horizons and green
exit signs ahead. Looks more like
Queen and Spadina on a silver screen.
The southeast corner, to be precise. With
coffee cup and legs, the moment
before you saw me across the way,
your lips crawling over the cardboard rim.
A world revealed in a glance. How'd
you manage all that? Only you in focus
on all the street.

In the next act, you're extricating
yourself from the Hacienda like Deborah
Kerr in Separate Tables, and later
sat gracious in the Rex accepting
plaudits and kudos justly deserved,
moving to your own beat while the band
went down to Rio in five-four time

And in the Italian restaurant, that thing
you did with your eyes just after you said
you're…head over…etcetera.
Garbo, the last minute of Camille,
didn't do it any better. No, wait
it was more like Bette Davis,

65

alley lights dancing in big eyes,
as she's about to turn away in Kid Galahad.
The big lug wants the good girl instead. Me?
You're more my type.

Yes, and you strutting barefoot
across blue linoleum just as you're
doing across my mind at midnight now, while
they play Imagination. It's funny
how I watch the world flicker and change
when you move your head or draw back
your knees.

Step off the screen
and come to me across
the darkened theatre, engrave
your autograph all over me,
yet another time

SOMEWHERE WEST OF MONTMARTRE

Eating up the kilometres
Two weeks of prairie roads
Grain elevator skylines
Gophers stand and watch me pass

Norweena, Ninette, Birtail and Beulah
Cutknife, Carry the Kettle
Keeseekoose and Cowersess

"Wish you'd of brought some of that
B.C. rain with you. Need
Plenty of it for a decent crop
And a decent crop won't hardly
Pay the bills."

Outskirt strips making inroads til
No more downtowns in big towns
And little towns are barely hanging on
Farmers sit over coffee at Subway
Chester Chicken came to Duck Lake
And I dreamed Poundmaker
Up all night in Robin's Doughnuts

Me, I'm still driving,
Driving. Poorman, Thunderchild,
Tramping Lake, Snowflake,
Live Long. Avoiding malls
And franchise eateries
As if they were metaphors
And similies

THE FERRY

Just now Cliff Wray
That squeeze box trucker
With his boys on spoons and mandolin
Is spinning a reel for Father
O'Flynn that priest
Who put antlers all over
His house down by Abrans Cove

Over in Port Aux Basque town
By the Subway in the Irving Store
A man found an astrolabe
From Portugal, dated 1628
Just today it was. Stumbled over it
In some rumrunner's cove
A day of white caps on teal water
Sky as blue as an amateur water colour
A day purloined from razor blade winds
And spider web mists

Cars and trucks are lined up
Like supplicants for pogey cheques
And from a trailer back of a Reo
Conventional one old cow, smarter
Than mates all contented, knows the slaughter
House lies on the other side of the water
His deep cries sound across the lot
To run around limestone hills
Lichen-stained, the colour of a butcher's apron
And keeps it up, drawn out
Blue moos, complete with bentnotes
And melismata, a mooed lament
To freeze sunny daytrippers and
Stop grown up truckers in their tracks

And you can try playing that
On your spoons sometime, by Jesus

SITTING BULL

"Rode him
around in a
buckboard. He
was a fat man. I
remember
his smell."

His bird-voice, disembodied
in the antlered brown lobby
of the Maple Creek Hotel. White
Stetson comic around shrunken
head. Just old talking bones
in a double-breasted suit.
Ninety-nine in 1970. Me nodding,
encouraging. In my mind,
arithme-ticing; he'd have been
eleven back in 1882
when he was companion
to the great Sitting Bull

"Used to
take him back
in the hills,
The Cypress
Hills there, to watch
the animals
that came to
the water to drink.
In town he
liked to
sit and
watch the young girls.

Young
white girls   younger
the better, just
come from church.
That Injun
smelled
like something wild."

ROAD GIRL

She looks impossible in boots
and summer shorts, huggable
in parka and mittens
lips red painted all year round
and saucy always in a yellow hard hat

It's a goddamned flag girl
with whom I'm smitten
No girl, really but a working woman
a real ball of fire
looks like Barbara Stanwyck

She makes me stop, slow and go
I sit there idling and obeying
her, envisioning toenails same
colour as her lips, snug
in white socks in lace-up boots.
Flag girl naked under
rubber rain slicker

Only once I've seen her off-duty
Just yesterday getting out
of a little red car, pale knit
dress, hem sliding up brown legs
She came into the store and looked
as if knowing, lips parting and
white teeth appearing
like a sign to proceed

Desa Finito

There goes old gape mouth, goofing
as I dreamed him in a zoot suit
the colour of polenta. Moths launched
from pockets made a confetti halo
around his bad haircut on Copertino's
cobblestones. A good gumshoe, I stayed
one block behind, waiting for anything
miraculous. Some crossed themselves
when he shuffled by snapping skinny fingers,
swinging his gold watch chain. Others
gave him the Bronx cheer and Crazy Joe
raspberried back. Cried Wynonie Harris-like:
"Hoy! Hoy!"
Then he awasn't there any more, not
behind that flagon pyramid of Puglia red
nor shielded by the fat lady's butterfly
skirts. It was as if Joey Desa lost his tail,
his Sam Sorry-Ass Spade which was me,
who'd now to slink back
to medieval office. Then I followed
a citizen's upraised arm and pointed finger,
spied the future saint and laughing stock
atop a gargoyle's head seven stories up.
Los Olvidados larrikins straight out of Open City
taunted him with photographs of the Virgin Mary,
out of focus but comely. My mind's eye
zoomed in as Joey groaned, face rictus-ridden,
eyeballs vanished and returned, and suddenly
he resembled Slim Gallard—cool, dark,
pencil-line moustache—and rose, a-routi
a-vouti, to fly above buildings and olive
orchards, blissful. And was last seen
heading in the general direction
of heaven.

REAL DOWN SYNDROME

Feathers on the front porch
and a little something red
and undigestible, all that
remains of a robin. The cat
looks guilty. Up on the road,
"Fuck you!" screamed
from an old red pickup truck
by a mufflerless child roaring
past ditches of fast food
trash. On the bus
a rheumy-eyed pair. He tries
to kiss her. She resists,
wrinkling a nose like a thumb.
"I thought you loved me," whines
the swain through saliva spray
and begins to cry. Meanwhile
scandals are breaking out
all over. Another massacre
in Africa. In the Globe
today, bad news for a deadman's
ticket, and I'm coming down
with the flu. At home, the wind
worries windows. I've
put towels at the bottom
of the door the wolf's the other
side of. There's a full moon tonight
and two whole bottles of rum. That
better do it.

INDIAN SUMMER

Sitting in chiaroscuro
Under a tree at Sunset Beach
Slim feet in late lingering sun
Leaves like crabs scuttle
on the first of October
She's rubbing lotion on spindly legs,
Spidery fingers with red nails,
plastic bracelets clattering
at her wrist. I nod
and we both smile.
Hers resigned, conscious
of vertical lines just revealed
above wide red mouth.
She must have been something
three or four decades ago.
The white bathing suit now
like a forgotten birthday present,
tangled in crepe paper
after the party.
I turn away. Silver
sailboats flutter on a sea gone
pink. The show-off orange sun
gathers up three Russian tankers
and takes its dive, mocking
her and me, and all the rest
of the bodies on the beach.

DROP DEAD GORGEOUS

Thirty-one years old
and at the top of her game
The nemeth of the neighborhoods
A mythic piece of street stuff
Untouchable
And hard as nails

Cockatrice of the barrooms,
She lays waste men with just a glance
And out on the pavement bull
dykes fall down like dominoes
when she goes strutting by

She's got predator eyes
And legs way up to there
Owns three Cadillacs
and every record Harry the Hipster
Gibson ever made. The only thing
She's lacking is any clue
She's not immortal. Heard
about it once but the girl
Wasn't having any

Someday she'll be a once
great beauty, gumming
her oatmeal, loosing
her bearings as well as
her slippers with no hard
high breasts to point the way
to the tv room

So laugh tall lovely one
Pavement pandrosos but
You're only thirty-one once
And no one's spared Not Garbo
even or Catherine the Great

Today a five-alarm frail
tomorrow a heap of ashes

I know even if you don't. So
Since we're here, my
semiramis of the streets,
Pull off your Johnsons, get
on your back on the floor
and just once tussle
with a mortal.

OH, LUCKY MAN

Autumny afternoon at Horseshoe Bay,
Waiting. The uniformed young captain's
Leaning on a rail and chatting up
A passenger. She has obvious eyes
For him—tall, well-salaried—and
He's not oblivious. I see pairs
Of silver scales, and weights and measures
In cartoon bubbles above each head
Against a rare blue sky

Back at the Troller Pub, two men
in hip waders with pitchers
And mugs, with bellies and beards,
Bragging of hockey triumphs on rinks
That have melted in everyone else's
Memory, and of more recent scores
With females just mad for their bodies.
Above them, Mario Lemieux's jersey
Nailed to the wall, stretched as if
a God had fled a crucifixion,
Six sixes skating over
Back and sleeves.

And what are former lovers saying about
Them, these fishermen? Or me, for that
Matter? I don't care. It's a brand new
Life. There's a long-legged
bottle-blond who has a beauty mark
at the bridge of her nose,
She knows things and spills
out of her clothes, and says
she feels that way too

Big big boats make waves
That approach and retreat
Tides confound chart compilers
The sea doesn't care

About you, my mermaid, or me
An eternal urchin. I'll tie you up
With long green strands of kelp
And drown in your big brown eyes

Whistles bleet and blast
out on the Sound
Like a band of mocking seals. My ship
Is pulling away from the harbour
Bound for who knows where.

HAYWIRE CHORUSES

He rises, sometimes tottering
but always sure-footed, from
tables in today's Railway
or Picadilly, as in boozecans
of yesteryear.
And as soon as his back is turned,
the character-collectors, the would-be
and never-were poets, start
scrapping over a stray alexandrine, a few
strophes that answer each other
like fours traded on his beer-soaked coaster

Who is that guy? They want to know
as he hits familiar bricks. "Him?"
says Full Bore Bill of a caulk boot
chorus. "Why that's one
who works a special alchemy and
deciphers fled yesterdays."

"Yes, and what's more," adds old
Grand Daddy Tough. "He's a fella
who's become more than the sum
of his empty bottles."

Watch him pass by.
Dig his kicks, his pleats
and his stride. Regard him owl-staring
into the million glitter.

Come on, I know the guy. We can talk
some trash. He's the rare, real goods
who didn't swallow his poetry in universities
but got it in kickaround camps and woods,
from bootleggers and bandits, and after
devouring his predecessors in bunkhouses
and skidrow hotels. Why, he got it
from the South Rim and the Elephant

Graveyard, at the volcano capital
and in the country of the Bull,
in Okalla and the Andy Devine Room.

This is no poet whose emotional life
is circumscribed by 500 square feet
of classroom. His arms encompassed more
than coeds. Rather there were
rye-roughed women, beanery queens
and one little Miss Tightbones.

So many assorted Sally's who
pedalled their hips
and sold short their dreams.

Who can forget the Marble Arch
and Annie, immortal in its corridors?
He was no moustachioed Lothario then
and Annie didn't give him any more than
earlier laundry ladies. But he saw
the light or lit the light
in many another's eyes, down through the days
before finding   his wild girl again.

You don't know who that is? This man who
recorded the concert of the grasses
and ripplings in the wind? Why, we've
dogged his heels in sinister seasons
to backwoods Saturday dances, along trails
where fireflies bobbed like flashlights
and dead folks whispered in the weeds.

We've followed the belted back of his benny
along tumbledown streets in the mousehours
and peered with his eyes
through Joe-sent-me peepholes
at a literature for grownups.

He broke down the doors and turned up
the saxophones, permitted us
to cut in on a tarantella
with Mae West McKersky
and the ghost of the club-footed girl.

Now they've swept out the riff-raff
and turned the ladderback chairs
over like hourglasses. He's the main
man remaining and it's time
to heel-and-toe it out of here.
Watch as once more off he goes
skywriting on apricot air,
the guy who knows   the secret
of Whispering Chester.

Take a look. Yeah, grapple
for that coaster. Tell
your grandchildren you saw
Pete Trower.

You Take the High Road

In an Acadian on the Lower Road
My car covered with other cars
(And ships, boats and planes).
Followed a stake truck hauling
Rabbits in this dream, green
Robins on the roadside verge,
Another Robyn chewing my ear
With pink lips and one red
Shoe. A van driven by two guys
With big hearts, runs
The stop sign at Joe Road.
Stake truck jams on air
Brakes too late, the bunny load
Shifts, woodside slats snap and rabbits
Make for macadam. Hundreds
Of hares, going every which
Goddamned way and multiplying
Sure as shit. Rabbit noses
Also pink, and the sky explodes
Dogs barking, bears beating
Their breasts. It's *Summertime*
On the radio: The living's fine.
If her daddy's rich take her
Out for a meal. I have my meal
On the naughahyde. Song ends,
Voice says: You are experiencing
A bona fide dada moment!
Pere Ubu's grinning iron
Pyrites in the shimmering sky
Over all of us
On the Lower Road.

IV

The Frost Giant

THE FROST GIANT

The clouds it says spit forth
unfortunate Ymir and his friend
a cow called Audhumbla
But there were as yet
no clouds as we shall see
Which makes for a big problem
in Scandinavian mythology

Ymir was slain by Odin,
Vili and Ve   who sound
like a tumbling team in old
Oslo vaudeville. Odin,
Vili and Ve

And from Ymir's body
was the world created.
His skull became the heavens
and his blood the sea
His brain made mountains
and his hair the trees.
The earth itself was fashioned
out of the eyebrows of Ymir
and that, if you care to think
about it—and not many do—
seems an unusual choice, for
What became of Ymir's skin
and Ymir's flesh?
Yet the eyebrow earth
is merely a pedant's puzzle
For consider the problem
of the clouds. Clouds formed
from the brain of He
Whom clouds spit forth.

And as for that cow,
Audhumbla, it
was never heard from again.

85

OLD CAT

Right here it was twenty-eight
Years ago on cheap aubergio cot
While she pencilled on eyeliner, legs
Straddling the bidet, singing Billie
Holiday, that I scribbled Palatine
Lines after seeing stray
Cats wandering in the Boboli.
Sleek, lean, grey and dangerous like
Weapons, keeping to the shadows,
To themselves, except to couple,
Hot and rough at the foot of famous walls

Now I am alone and what became of you?
The cats too are gone.
Not chased out of town to prowl the edges
Of the autostrada but eradicated
By an edict approved in a municipal hall
That was ancient in the Renaissance

This time I cross the river
By the bridge at Via de Tornabuoni
And look over at the back of Benvenuto
Cellini and thousands of Germans.
Someone's voice lesson I hear
From that high window and that
Campanile. A mezzo soprano
Just like the one who made
Her ablutions while I scribbled Palatine
Lines in 1971. I've had a few good turns
Around this globe since then. Earned
My grizzle and patina. Become
In fact that old stray
With scars and serrated ear. The only one
Now wandering
In the Boboli Gardens

SUNDAY IN GREENLAND

I went on a boat ride
one early morning in August,
there being so little else
in little Nuuk to do.
Drinks were served
to me and a dozen Danes.
They in blue nylon windbreakers.
We sped along a wild coast,
Put ashore at the foot
of a great iron hill. I climbed
while Danes took pictures on the beach.
Crushed lichens like rust and yellow paint.
At the top, turning away from the sea,
I found the brief summer hiding
place of ice and snow

There were more drinks, returning.
I didn't know what they were saying.
It was afternoon before we got back.
Two old men dragged part of a whale carcass
along a street of Copenhagen apartment houses
Beyond them in clear blue harbour waters
were skulls of icebergs.
On a hill in back of Nuuk,
I came upon a wedding.
The Inuit bride and groom waved
from wooden steps in a blizzard
of rice and confetti.
At the back of the church were green
hills, dark greenland hills, planted
with white crosses, that rolled
all the way down
to the sea

SOLUTION TOMORROW

*poem made from The Guardian (Europe) crossword while on
Firenze-Zurich train, car #8, seat 96, September 22, '99*

Across

Fame of the new owner never
ever diminished after taking up
with that round black cat. Timber
supplier in blue seeks to marry
current rubbish, rejected
by entertainer. Firm backs her
working with earth and pasting in
a variety of wide privet some joker
removed. Something was allowed
to spoil you, grand home girl.
Try folding one slowly, further.
Takes long time making spectacular
display. Caught volunteers taking
it back to room. Something ape-like
climbs always on U.S. soldier's back.
An atrium. I rebuilt an
atrium. Dope having lost pipe studies
China.

Down

Twisted ropes need no core
Cut up a large amount
of your companion but failing
to take snooker ball back
is erratic. Scoundrel brings mother
in white and swaggers around
that first sailing vessel.
Sure, enter into arrangement
for custody but push that
not. A brown pair cutting
teacher up. The cabbage
gaped, disturbed
by a topless vicar.
Rogue goes to film studio
for wowing. Master sits in seat
mauls poor youth leader
in shelter. Once dispersed,
confused padre Bill caught taking
journalist around compass points.
It's irritating but
I was yours
at one time

My Romanian Family

It was up in the Carpathians,
Down in an ash grove of burnt
skeleton pines. They made
a raggle-taggle band, five
excitable rom and one brown blasé bear

They open their bag of tired
tricks when the gadja humping
his blooey hoves into view
down the long renaissance road.
Don silk scarves and hoop
earrings, start shuffling the decks

"Want your driveway blacktopped?" one
man asks. "Cheap?" "I don't
have a driveway," I tell him. "How
about a little three-card monte?" The other
queries while the woman ducks under
a wagon of old gaudy colours
and watches me between the spokes.

The men hate each other because
of her. The little girl kisses the bear
who smells like the corpse of a fat man
dead in a river. Flies are eating
his nose. The little boy is blind.
The men offer the woman to me, also
at a reduced rate. And when
I shake my head they point
to the little girl and then the boy
"He'll never recognize you later."

Because that doesn't work they
tell me I need a bottle
of this ancient almond elixir
that looks like milk of magnesia and'll
put lead in a dead man's pencil

Well then how about this stone
carving found in a cave right here
in the deepest Carpathians, done by
a gypsy ancestor before he left
to go awandering. They shouldn't really
sell it, it being part of their proud
heritage, don't you know.

Well eventually they accepted me
after I showed them how to make
tin pots pass for copper. They
stood me to a drink and soon I fell
asleep watching the orange alligators,
under a sky like dice on a horse blanket

I woke when they started killing
each other with long dull knives. The woman
took refuge under my blanket, and we
buried them next morning   before
hitting the road, and after rifling
their pockets.

So we drifted for many months my
new family unit and me, leading
the bear by the nose. Stealing chickens
and turning tin pots to copper. I
breathed fire, the little girl
looked sad and the boy was always good
for a kopeck or a couple of quid. And
Esmeralda told everybody's fortune
but our own.

At night, kids asleep on spruce bough
beds, she demanded increasingly unusual
sex while alligators watched, and made
gypsy sounds in the Carpathian night

I left them somewhere near Tirana

The woman never said a word. The little
girl cried, the boy waved once
in the wrong direction and the bear
followed me as far
as the edge of the clearing.

LETTER HOME

Well, sweetheart, here I am
in another two-bit town tottering
over the edge of the earth, smack dab
in the middle
of the Wallace Line. It
might be Brazil or Indonesia,
East Africa just as easily
Three woebegone blocks long
from a harbour to the only bar.
There's a dead-legged woman follows
me on my route from one to
the other, dragging herself on hands
hard as hoofs, head turned toward me, leering
Her name's Mahdi or Maria, and
an old brindle bitch dogs her
heels, dragging flattened nipples over broken
ground. Now and again it'll growl at nothing
in particular or at life in general. She
always wears a dress, the dead-legged
woman, and it always rides
up to her rear. The bad part
is   it's not a bad-looking rear and she's not
a bad-looking woman. "What's worse," says
the commandante, blinking his superating eye,
"She'll get a hell of a lot better-looking soon."

He reminds me of an Arkansas-Islamic state trooper.
"And that's when I'll nab you," he adds, making
the international thumb and forefinger gesture
for mordida.

I can't flee this place til the new propellor
arrives from Manaus or Surabaya. It's been
three weeks already, holed up in a hole
in the wall room where I lie and sweat
There's a ceiling fan but the weight of indefinable
dead things has overburdened the motor. The toilet's

in the yard, graffiti reads, "the bartender's
in love with my ass." The fellow
in question sports a scar from temple
to chin. "Only took one man to carve up his face,"
the dead-legged lady told me. "But four big men
had to hold him down."

"Come on," I wondered out loud over my arak
and my pisco. "How bad
can the dude be?"

"Well boss," interjected the dwarf. "They say
he did time with Sonny Liston. And that Sonny
was his punk."

Sometimes I dose myself with quinine
and go sit on the dock of the bay. Water's
the colour of flour gravy. Fat rats float
by on their backs like vacationers, eyes
like marbles in a taxidermist's tray

Some joker named her restaurant
the Biafra Buffet. I've had a glimpse
of the kitchen but I eat there anyway
dedicated as I am to the spirit
of scientific enquiry, and wondering
what in the world might be hiding
in the bread or come crawling out of the soup

Did I mention I have a rash and that nobody
here sells immodium? The fellow
on the postage stamp is hydrocephalic,
there's the constant threat of a coup
and the only thing to read is Margaret Atwood?

The commandante's son spends all day everyday
in the park—which is a bare earth doggy
bathroom with four dead palm trees—staring
at pictures of mini-vans and abusing himself

I don't think I can take it another minute, baby.

Hold on, there's a knocking on the door.

Two days later: Listen, this won't be easy
We had a policy, you and me, to always
tell each other the truth. Well, it
was Mahdi-Maria knocking, down low
on the door. Said she had something
to show me and she did, and I guess
I'm going to be staying
in this two-bit town at the end
of the world, me
and the dead-legged lady
She says she was made for me
and this is the kind of place
where I belong

ORANGE WALK

In Orange Walk I'm waiting
for the Batty Bus. Going by—
swaying trucks with cut cane loads
on broken streets. Import-Export
CDs for Sale. I'm fancy
free, I'm Duty Free.
The joyeria's not a whorehouse.
Crumbling Public Works await
some other administration. Rooftop
gardens sprout fronds of rebar palms
Rainbow piles of underpants
in market stalls. Vans full
of evangelists. Mennonites too
in bonnets and black overalls
just arrived, purse-lipped, jug-earred
in OW Town, like back home in moonshine
mountains. Blacks Indians Syrians Indians
Chinese Creole Garfuna speak a sidewalk
dipthong doubletalk all night long
to a mambo reggae Rudi Vallee crooner beat
Roosters squawk by chicken wire fences
with red blooms of morning glory.
In the waterlily shallows
A white flamingo still
as a lawn ornament
among lavender flower tops, orange
beak to the breeze that ruffles
bamboo shoots.   Down
by the river
I'm waiting
for the Batty Bus.
For to take me
far away from here.

96

GOING HOME BLUES

Blue-pink singing curly bill
Bird in the spreading
Traveller's Tree,
Me in banyan roots hidey hole
Got to get up from the fine
Coral sand, fly back
To a land beyond
The light. Say good-bye
To crotons and causarinas
Go wear clothes and overcoats
Pay hydro bills, hide
Under Hudson Bay blankets
Need to find a job, hoard
Prime Ministers and, maybe
In a few years, come back,
If I'm lucky.

My colour will fade.
No parrot green sea
In my rainy harbour nor
Nights of drum throb
Safe there I'll be from
Falling coconuts if not
Drive-by shooters
And shopping mall hooligans

The blue-pink curly bill
Bird mocks me in
The spreading Traveller's Tree,
Singing: Woe-he.
Woe-he Hee hee!

V

The Fix Is In

THE FIX IS IN

You didn't ask for the bout.
No one else
Ever did either. And only
Mystics post odds.
The crowd bides its time
Like an animal,
Some jeering, some weeping,
Most numb. The ref
Is blind and wears a skull cap.
At ringside attendants
Wait wisecracking
To toss what remains
Down the memory chute.

At least, you answered
The bell for the first.
Billions don't.
Yet until that first knockdown
You weren't even aware
Of the Opponent's presence.
And so you've been permitted a few rounds
By turns toddling, gawky, deluded,
Pathetically hopeful,
Tired.   The Opponent
Toys with you between hurts,
And waits his pleasure,
The age-old one of spilling your guts
And gouging out your eyes. Waits
To smack you a thousand
Unanswered blows.
The Opponent knows all the tricks
For he invented them. You'll
Be overwhelmed by a flurry
Of hooks and jabs and double-
Crosses. His combinations
Are impeccable, the
Sucker punch inevitable. Soon,

Soon enough begins the
blind ref's numbers,
The Long Count from which
There's been no rising.
And all the while,
The girls with the roundcards parade,
Marking time in long legs
And balloon breasts
Of crumbling flesh

BROTHER AND SISTER ACT

He came on real mild
but it was just a front
He was foreign-influenced, up
to no good. El Nino
took out the bridge,
Left the government stranded
on the other side, and you couldn't
blame it on the bossa nova.
He warmed his way
onto your picket line
Turned up at city council meetings, got
appointed to the library board
That boy didn't horse around
He infiltrated television,
the movie industry. During
secret meetings he hid
under the couch with lost pink mules

Remember the El Nino hearings?
Are you now or
have you ever been
a Nino? Did you ever knowingly
give succour to Ninos? Give us
the names of every Nino
you've ever known.

Ah, the poor kid wasn't always a threat
Started out a trifle breezy perhaps
But he had to take the rap
for ever hokey hurricane and two bit tornado
to hit the coast so it's not surprising
he got a little hot
under the collar
and started to blow
El Nino slinked around schoolyards preying
on other ninos. Posing
as a priest, a scout leader, a pillar

of the community. El Nino monitored
the internet. He was a wet blanket
who liked to mess around.

But you didn't mess with the boy
or he turned your guts to water,
ruined your ski trip and lay
waste the crops, made you
row to the barn on the National News
He might have blown you away, it didn't
matter, the kid didn't give a shit.

The boy could lower the Panama
Canal and make Greenland green
Melt the snowcap and the ice
in your Caesar not to mention your heart
First, you swore you were mad about him
But soon enough he made those brown eyes
blue and tears flow like
swollen rivers. El Nino was best
at beguiling, by whistling up the glades
but, oh ye gades, don't be fooled
For it's no good at all he blew

Now, experts say El Nino's finally headed south
but they also claim he has a sister
Not some mild chinookie neither, no
this one's real cool, La Nina
Sired by an icicle and the Dairy
Queen, born under a snowberry bush,
polar ice for cloche cap
La Nina's going to introduce
snow shoes to Suva. They'll soon
be ice huts in Indonesia and Polar
bear swims in Java in June.

And so it begins all over again...

Are you now or have you ever been

a Nina?
Give us the names of every Nina
you've ever known.

THE PRETTIEST GIRL FROM MEXICO, MAINE

She's lying in an Ipswich garden
Back by the compost pile
The prettiest girl from Mexico, Maine
It was quite a shock to the boy
Who found her   while running down
A long pop fly, dancing through beds
Of impatiens, skirting lacy hydrangea
The white ball hanging up there
For a blue moment before its fall
And rolling to rest
By the radius
And ulna that looked
To be made of papier mache

She'd always seemed foreign, though
Born there. Too much for that little town
And everyone knew it was true. Winter
Nights reading books about faraway places
Summer walking on dancer's legs, a honey blonde
To the edge of that berg. And saw
Herself an old lady by the
Welcome to Mexico sign
She wanted more than to go with a gaggle
Of girls shopping in Skowhegan or to
Wild weekends at Old Orchard Beach
So when the man in the town car
Pulled over and opened the door—the interior
All silvery soft leather; he was handsome,
Such a friendly smile—she got in
And the two of them drove off laughing
To Boston and the whole wide world

There are still blond hairs
Among weeds growing out of her skull
The death mask grimace shows a couple
Of teeth. And look at the swiss cheese
Holes in a skirt hiked way up

On those skeleton legs. She doesn't look
Peaceful or pretty at all lying there
Dead in an Ipswich garden
Back by by the compost pile
the prettiest girl from Mexico, Maine

LAUGHING AT LIFE

On the little Saturday stage
playing my part, I told
about you, birthday
girl, leaving out lines
concerning your broken body,
the perfume behind your knees.
After the briefest
moment, they applauded
all but one woman
whose nervous giggle burst
into all-out laughter
and wise-ass me bantered
back, yet later fretted
in the darkened parking lot
At the disrespect of it, imagined
our roles reversed, you
laughing in back of murdered me
and being ogled too
for you'd here a middle-aged
beauty be, I bet.
Perhaps you know all this already
and forgive, unless into nothingness
you've really gone. Vanished
like tender creased flesh
at backs of knees themselves.
And on my side
of the curtain,
this
for a fleeting
hour only.

If She Were You
(Anniversary Girl)

Now come to screaming scenes
In restaurants Her face twisted
into hideous mask of belittlement
               But her alive, at least,
in laneways.
Yet what if it were she
found broken on Mexican street
and you still among the living?
We'd laugh, and dance,
two happy shades, and fall
lovers' limbs entangled
in crazy erotic sleep, this night
thirtieth anniversary
of your first night
in the ground

Or would promises have been done in
by quotidian killers, and you
become she, who I nursed and tried to love
You in the hideous borrowed mask
bellicose in an everyday
devil's voice

WITHOUT MUSIC…WITHOUT DANCERS… WITHOUT ANYTHING

The face on the cover
of the ballet book. Could
it be?…Yes, yes…It's
him. It's…the bogey man
himself, I declare…should have
kept him locked up…How curious
though…he almost looks,
well…if one didn't know all
about him…one might say
his expression is rather
saintly…I know it sounds
silly, considering who we're
speaking of here…mean, vicious
anti-Semitic bastard…and all
that…but…the way he's
staring…up like that…makes one
think of a penitent in a
religious painting…It's like
he's looking toward God…or, at
some heavenly dance…the ballet
he's always on about…Don't be
fooled…see, it's a ruse…the
old ballet ruse…Death owns
all the cafes, indeed…He'll rip out
your heart, sell you up the river
before you can say…Robinson
But…those angel eyes…They're
really madman's eyes…it's all
been documented…He needs a shave
long whiskers in the vertical
groove tween nose and mouth
Scrawny neck…head delicate
really…What crazy brain
behind corduroy forehead…the
hair, pencil lines that might

have been scrawled by an outsider
artist...Adolf Wolfi...someone
mad as he is...see the ratty
scarf? Probably picked it out
of an ash bin...in
the Zone...Menilimontant...they
had cholera there...syphilis...It
was worth your life to venture
places like that...Of course,
this all was going on
when he could still practice
Before...he lost...his
license...and his mind...Those
things he wrote...and him
from a good family...his mother
made lace...he went to school
in England...fat lot of good
it did him...To the dungeon
with him...keep him in the castle,
lock the iron doors...alligators
in the moat! Be careful...But still
that look!...The expression
on the face of Celine...As if...
as if he's...about
to proclaim his love...for the entire
human race, Jews included...Now
that would be embarrasssing, eh?
As if he's just seen through a rent
in the curtain...got a glimpse, yes,
of the other side...But don't
be fooled...We know who we're
dealing with...the photo...
look close...it doesn't lie...Even
though it's probably been
doctored...if you'll pardon
the expression...Remember it's him
No other....evil Louis...Celine...it's
not even his real name...And what're
the last words of the last

ballet in the book his face
is on the cover of?…"I'll
make mince meat of the lot of you!
        Curtain."

SCARY NIGHTS

Any fallen woman or man jack
of us will tell you there
was a crescent moon romantic
as all get-out where now that
rusty scythe sits ready to slip.
It made promises
(the moon)
it never intended to keep.

Now prisoners of illusions
and lammisters, harpies
harpooned by a one-legged lover,
prodigals all, all've come home to roost.
We sleep on a brown carpet, there's
a jungle gym and coloured condoms
in the dried up pool, and last month's
black leaves where poi flashed
in July. We keep shortdogs for companions
and swallow brown bag memories. I kissed you
in the all together, never
took precautions. Now I'd gladly press
chapped lips to your furbelow.
Here I see only trees naked and when the wind blows
they all have tourette's syndrome. It's forty below
on a scary night.

They're all scary nights.

Man Overboard

I

Your ship is due
in the outer harbour
when the sun goes down.
With a flashlight from the porthole,
you'll signal all's clear and much more.
Four dusky lads row me out.
Their naked wahines dump petals
on my head and give me
garlands for my girl.
I'll climb love's bull kelp
ladder of lust. You'll cover
my body with mango
kisses and squeeze my head between
your breasts so I won't see
tears of joy, or you mine
Your aureoles contain multitudes
As I work my way down
a foot and a half you'll murmur
in multitudes, gasp endearments
Thank whomever we found each other
By then they'll have slipped,
anchor, and we, you and me, will be
adrift on a pink Sargasso Sea
of lust and love, under
our lucky stars.

II

Your ship is due
in the outer harbour
at dusk but it foundered
getting out of the locks
Or the guy on the bridge
with the flags signalled
the wharfinger, "Forget it!"
Or you sent me a letter
from Paramaraibo with
an invitation to your wedding
Or the ship arrived and you
didn't signal so I climbed
the bull kelp ladder only to be
speared by the second mate's
triton. Or was the first mate
your main enamorata? The ABs
and the ordinaries, they all
knew your name and the captain
had it tattooed on his manly chest

With nothing left to do, I doggy-
paddled back, nibbled by whelks,
collapsed on a beach of tin cans
and condoms, CD ROMS and dodo guano
Or more likely I stowed away
in a lifeboat, just a fool
under canvas and heard the trill
of your laughter, and the tinkle
of highball glasses. Peeked through
the portal of your stateroom
and saw you are still partial
to the position with a pillow
under your hips and your toes
pointed at the lucky stars

REMEMBRANCE DAY

Poll indicates desire for stronger defensive
capabilities. More destroyers,
bombers, missiles needed

Me, I wonder who's buried beneath
soldiers' bones in Flanders Field

Quick: Who fought the Hundred Years War?
Was the War of the Roses anything
but a bad movie? What the hell
was that Franco-Prussian thing about?

Ten thousand buddhists
with begging bowls
on the moonlight road
of 1310.

Which was first to rise
and flourish
and expire? Olmec,
Toltec or Aztec?

Did Etruscans have insomnia
same as me?

The lives of entire generations
of women and men make up
but a few lines in the palimpsest
of the Great Spirit.

From tree tops and belfries
Through the skies of my dreams,
falling ass over tea kettle,
all the snipers of history

What constituted paleolithic
pillow talk?

Into the Stein River Valley cave,
we tumbled eager for our love
and loved, and only then,
sated, saw three deer on the wall
Who drew the deer family?

You who are
in charge: stick your
stealth bombers up your ass
Go fuck yourself with your polls
and politics.

That's you and me, my sweet,
spooning skeletons of Nagasaki.

TIME'S DELICIOUS RIVER

after Ludwig Zeller

All birds fly
All doors give
All silence falls
As snow

You open up
And reality strips from eyelids
A life known
Only to you

Windows are open
In the gorges of the moon
And they mirror pity
When you cry

All faces the same,
Grief stricken, echoing
the heart
Let me drink

Now all is quiet here
Where? In the grey house
The wind having erased
the white peasant from my dreams